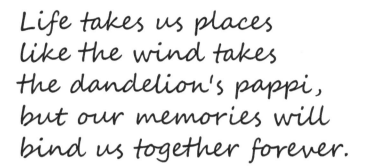

Life takes us places
like the wind takes
the dandelion's pappi,
but our memories will
bind us together forever.

ISBN 978-1-737550006

www.dandelionmemories.com

Thank you for being my friend!

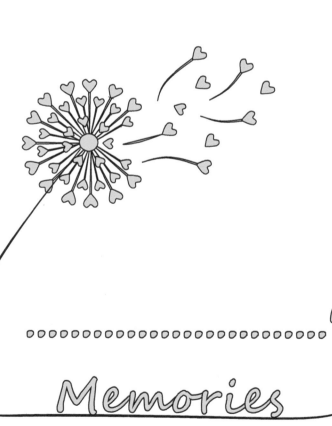

................................'s

Memories

INSTRUCTIONS

How to use this book ...

The owner of the book fills out these pages 4-5

The friends fill out these pages 6-53

The grown-ups fill out these pages 54-59

Write your name on the Birthday Calendar 60-61

Add your finger print to the Dandelion 62

This book belongs to:

_____

I am:

1 2 3 4 5 6 7 years old.

My hair is ☐ (color)

My eyes are ☐ (color)

I live in _____

My favorite food is _____

My favorite ice cream is

_____

I want to be _____

_____ when I grow up!

My favorite color is:

(color)

My favorite animal is:

(Draw yours)

My favorite thing to play with is:

(Draw yours)

A drawing of my family and me:

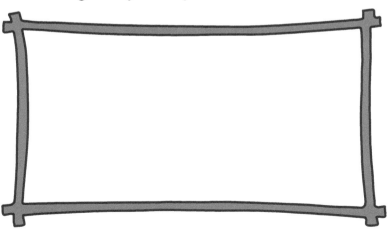

Today's date: _____

My name is:

_____

Photo

I am :

1 2 3 4 5 6 7 years old.

My hair is ☐ (color)

My eyes are ☐ (color)

We have known each other:

Since _____

From _____

We do fun things together like:

_____

_____

My favorite color is:

(color)

My favorite animal is:

(Draw yours)

My favorite thing to play with is:

(Draw yours)

A drawing from me to you:

Today's date: _____

My name is:

_____

Photo

I am :

1 2 3 4 5 6 7 years old.

My hair is ▢ (color)

My eyes are ▢ (color)

We have known each other:

Since _____

From _____

We do fun things together like:

_____

_____

My favorite color is:

(color)

My favorite animal is:

(Draw yours)

My favorite thing to play with is:

(Draw yours)

A drawing from me to you:

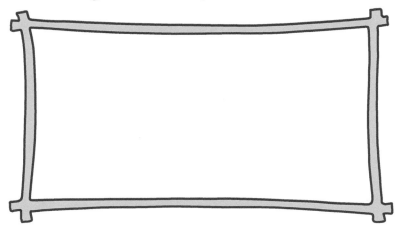

Today's date: _____

My name is:

_____

Photo

I am :

1 2 3 4 5 6 7 years old.

My hair is [ ] (color)

My eyes are [ ] (color)

We have known each other:

Since _____

From _____

We do fun things together like:

_____

_____

My favorite color is:

(color)

My favorite animal is:

(Draw yours)

My favorite thing to play with is:

(Draw yours)

A drawing from me to you:

Today's date: _____

My name is:

_____

Photo

I am :

1 2 3 4 5 6 7 years old.

My hair is [ ] (color)

My eyes are [ ] (color)

We have known each other:

Since _____

From _____

We do fun things together like:

_____

_____

My favorite color is:

(color)

My favorite animal is:

(Draw yours)

My favorite thing to play with is:

(Draw yours)

A drawing from me to you:

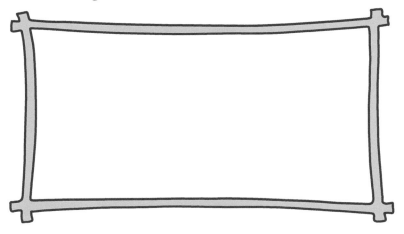

Today's date: _____

My name is:

_____

Photo

I am :

1 2 3 4 5 6 7 years old.

My hair is ☐ (color)

My eyes are ☐ (color)

We have known each other:

Since _____

From _____

We do fun things together like:

_____

_____

My favorite color is:

(color)

My favorite animal is:

(Draw yours)

My favorite thing to play with is:

(Draw yours)

A drawing from me to you:

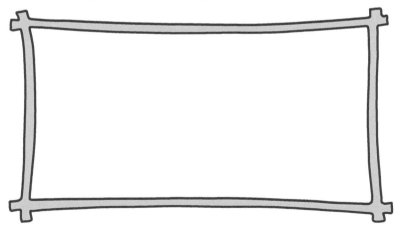

Today's date: _____

My name is:

_____

Photo

I am :

1 2 3 4 5 6 7 years old.

My hair is ⬜ (color)

My eyes are ⬜ (color)

We have known each other:

Since _____

From _____

We do fun things together like:

_____

_____

16

My favorite color is:

(color)

My favorite animal is:

(Draw yours)

My favorite thing to play with is:

(Draw yours)

A drawing from me to you:

Today's date: _____

My name is:

_____

I am :

1 2 3 4 5 6 7 years old.

My hair is [ ] (color)

My eyes are [ ] (color)

We have known each other:

Since _____

From _____

We do fun things together like:

_____

_____

My favorite color is:

(color)

My favorite animal is:

(Draw yours)

My favorite thing to play with is:

(Draw yours)

A drawing from me to you:

Today's date: _____

My name is:

_____

Photo

I am :

1 2 3 4 5 6 7 years old.

My hair is ☐ (color)

My eyes are ☐ (color)

We have known each other:

Since _____

From _____

We do fun things together like:

_____

_____

My favorite color is:

(color)

My favorite animal is:

(Draw yours)

My favorite thing to play with is:

(Draw yours)

A drawing from me to you:

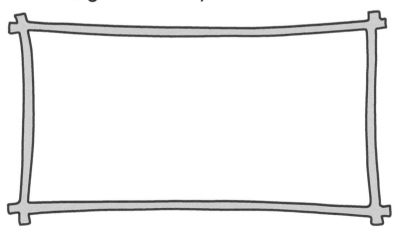

Today's date: _____

My name is:

_____

Photo

I am :

1 2 3 4 5 6 7 years old.

My hair is [   ] (color)

My eyes are [   ] (color)

We have known each other:

Since _____

From _____

We do fun things together like:

_____

_____

My favorite color is:

(color)

My favorite animal is:

(Draw yours)

My favorite thing to play with is:

(Draw yours)

A drawing from me to you:

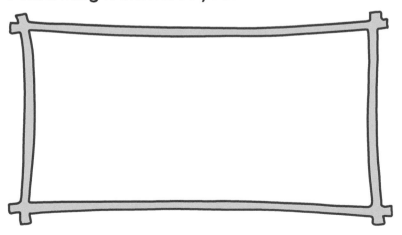

Today's date: _____

My name is:

_____

Photo

I am :

1 2 3 4 5 6 7 years old.

My hair is ☐ (color)

My eyes are ☐ (color)

We have known each other:

Since _____

From _____

We do fun things together like:

_____

_____

My favorite color is:

(color)

My favorite animal is:

(Draw yours)

My favorite thing to play with is:

(Draw yours)

A drawing from me to you:

Today's date: _____

My name is:

_____

Photo

I am :

1 2 3 4 5 6 7 years old.

My hair is ☐ (color)

My eyes are ☐ (color)

We have known each other:

Since _____

From _____

We do fun things together like:

_____

_____

My favorite color is:

(color)

My favorite animal is:

(Draw yours)

My favorite thing to play with is:

(Draw yours)

A drawing from me to you:

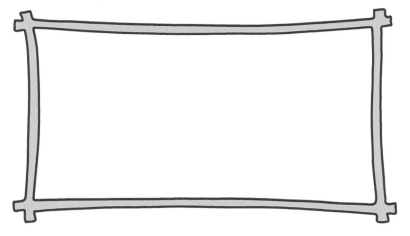

Today's date: _____

My name is:

_____

Photo

I am :

1 2 3 4 5 6 7 years old.

My hair is [ ] (color)

My eyes are [ ] (color)

We have known each other:

Since _____

From _____

We do fun things together like:

_____

_____

My favorite color is:

(color)

My favorite animal is:

(Draw yours)

My favorite thing to play with is:

(Draw yours)

A drawing from me to you:

Today's date: _____

My name is:

_____

Photo

I am :

1 2 3 4 5 6 7 years old.

My hair is ☐ (color)

My eyes are ☐ (color)

We have known each other:

Since _____

From _____

We do fun things together like:

_____

_____

My favorite color is:

(color)

My favorite animal is:

(Draw yours)

My favorite thing to play with is:

(Draw yours)

A drawing from me to you:

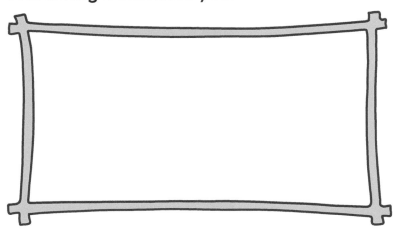

Today's date: _____

My name is:

_____

I am :

1 2 3 4 5 6 7 years old.

My hair is [ ] (color)

My eyes are [ ] (color)

We have known each other:

Since _____

From _____

We do fun things together like:

_____

_____

My favorite color is:

(color)

My favorite animal is:

(Draw yours)

My favorite thing to play with is:

(Draw yours)

A drawing from me to you:

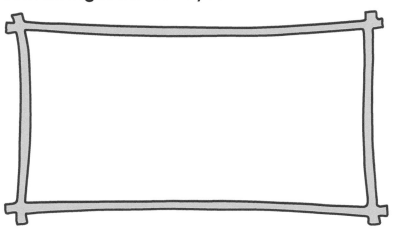

Today's date: _____

My name is:

_____

Photo

I am :

1 2 3 4 5 6 7 years old.

My hair is ☐ (color)

My eyes are ☐ (color)

We have known each other:

Since _____

From _____

We do fun things together like:

_____

_____

My favorite color is:

(color)

My favorite animal is:

(Draw yours)

My favorite thing to play with is:

(Draw yours)

A drawing from me to you:

Today's date: _____

My name is:

_____

I am :

1 2 3 4 5 6 7 years old.

My hair is [ ] (color)

My eyes are [ ] (color)

We have known each other:

Since _____

From _____

We do fun things together like:

_____

_____

My favorite color is:

(color)

My favorite animal is:

(Draw yours)

My favorite thing to play with is:

(Draw yours)

A drawing from me to you:

Today's date: _____

My name is:

_____

I am :

1 2 3 4 5 6 7 years old.

My hair is ☐ (color)

My eyes are ☐ (color)

We have known each other:

Since _____

From _____

We do fun things together like:

_____

_____

My favorite color is:

(color)

My favorite animal is:

(Draw yours)

My favorite thing to play with is:

(Draw yours)

A drawing from me to you:

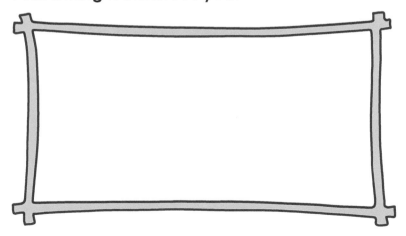

Today's date: _____

My name is:

_____

Photo

I am :

1 2 3 4 5 6 7 years old.

My hair is ☐ (color)

My eyes are ☐ (color)

We have known each other:

Since _____

From _____

We do fun things together like:

_____

_____

My favorite color is:

(color)

My favorite animal is:

(Draw yours)

My favorite thing to play with is:

(Draw yours)

A drawing from me to you:

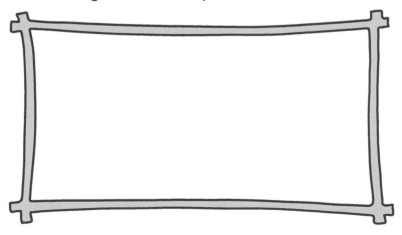

Today's date: _____

My name is:

_____

Photo

I am :

1 2 3 4 5 6 7 years old.

My hair is [ ] (color)

My eyes are [ ] (color)

We have known each other:

Since _____

From _____

We do fun things together like:

_____

_____

My favorite color is:

(color)

My favorite animal is:

(Draw yours)

My favorite thing to play with is:

(Draw yours)

A drawing from me to you:

Today's date: _____

My name is:

_____

Photo

I am :

1234567 years old.

My hair is ☐ (color)

My eyes are ☐ (color)

We have known each other:

Since _____

From _____

We do fun things together like:

_____

_____

My favorite color is:

(color)

My favorite animal is:

(Draw yours)

My favorite thing to play with is:

(Draw yours)

A drawing from me to you:

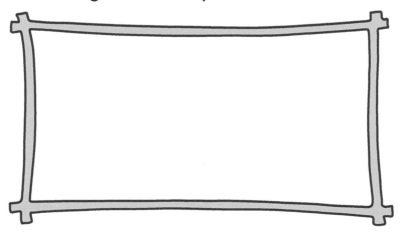

Today's date: _____

My name is:

_____

Photo

I am :

1 2 3 4 5 6 7 years old.

My hair is ☐ (color)

My eyes are ☐ (color)

We have known each other:

Since _____

From _____

We do fun things together like:

_____

_____

My favorite color is:

(color)

My favorite animal is:

(Draw yours)

My favorite thing to play with is:

(Draw yours)

A drawing from me to you:

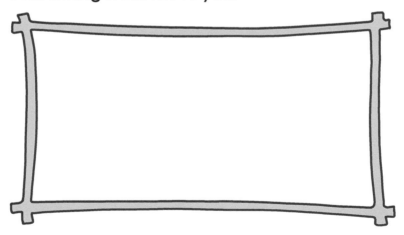

Today's date: _____

My name is:

_____

Photo

I am :

1 2 3 4 5 6 7 years old.

My hair is ☐ (color)

My eyes are ☐ (color)

We have known each other:

Since _____

From _____

We do fun things together like:

_____

_____

My favorite color is:

(color)

My favorite animal is:

(Draw yours)

My favorite thing to play with is:

(Draw yours)

A drawing from me to you:

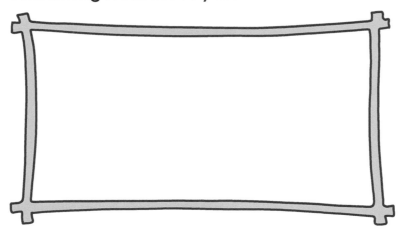

Today's date: _____

My name is:

_____

Photo

I am :

1 2 3 4 5 6 7 years old.

My hair is ☐ (color)

My eyes are ☐ (color)

We have known each other:

Since _____

From _____

We do fun things together like:

_____

_____

My favorite color is:

(color)

My favorite animal is:

(Draw yours)

My favorite thing to play with is:

(Draw yours)

A drawing from me to you:

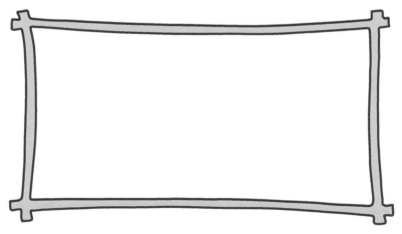

Today's date: _____

My name is:

_____

Photo

I am :

1 2 3 4 5 6 7 years old.

My hair is [ ] (color)

My eyes are [ ] (color)

We have known each other:

Since _____

From _____

We do fun things together like:

_____

_____

My favorite color is:

(color)

My favorite animal is:

(Draw yours)

My favorite thing to play with is:

(Draw yours)

A drawing from me to you:

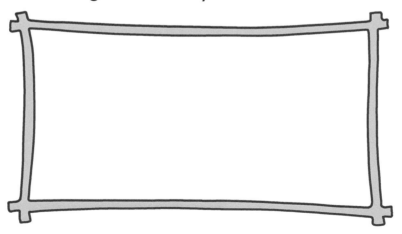

Today's date: _____

I am your

_____

My name is

_____

Photo

I was born in _____ (city, country)

My hair is _____ (color)

My eyes are _____ (color)

My favorite color is _____

My favorite food is _____

My favorite thing to do is _____

Something I really like about you is _____

_____

_____

Today's date: _____

I am your

_____

My name is

_____

I was born in _____ (city, country)

My hair is _____ (color)

My eyes are _____ (color)

My favorite color is _____

My favorite food is _____

My favorite thing to do is _____

Something I really like about you is _____

_____

_____

Today's date : _____

I am your

_____

My name is

_____

Photo

I was born in _____ (city, country)

My hair is _____ (color)

My eyes are _____ (color)

My favorite color is_____

My favorite food is _____

My favorite thing to do is _____

Something I really like about you is _____

_____

_____

Today's date : _____

I am your

_____

My name is

_____

Photo

I was born in _____ (city, country)

My hair is _____ (color)

My eyes are _____ (color)

My favorite color is _____

My favorite food is _____

My favorite thing to do is _____

Something I really like about you is _____

_____

_____

Today's date : _____

I am your

_____

My name is

_____

Photo

I was born in _____ (city, country)

My hair is _____ (color)

My eyes are _____ (color)

My favorite color is _____

My favorite food is _____

My favorite thing to do is _____

Something I really like about you is _____

_____

_____

Today's date : _____

I am your

_____

My name is

_____

Photo

I was born in _____ (city, country)

My hair is_____(color)

My eyes are_____(color)

My favorite color is _____

My favorite food is _____

My favorite thing to do is _____

Something I really like about you is _____

_____

_____

Today's date :_____

BIRTHDAY CALENDAR

Write your name and birthday in your birth month for me to remember!

January

_____
_____
_____
_____
_____

February

_____
_____
_____
_____
_____

March

_____
_____
_____
_____
_____

April

_____
_____
_____
_____
_____

May

_____
_____
_____
_____
_____

June

_____
_____
_____
_____
_____

BIRTHDAY CALENDAR

July

_____
_____
_____
_____
_____

August

_____
_____
_____
_____
_____

September

_____
_____
_____
_____
_____

October

_____
_____
_____
_____
_____

November

_____
_____
_____
_____
_____

December

_____
_____
_____
_____
_____

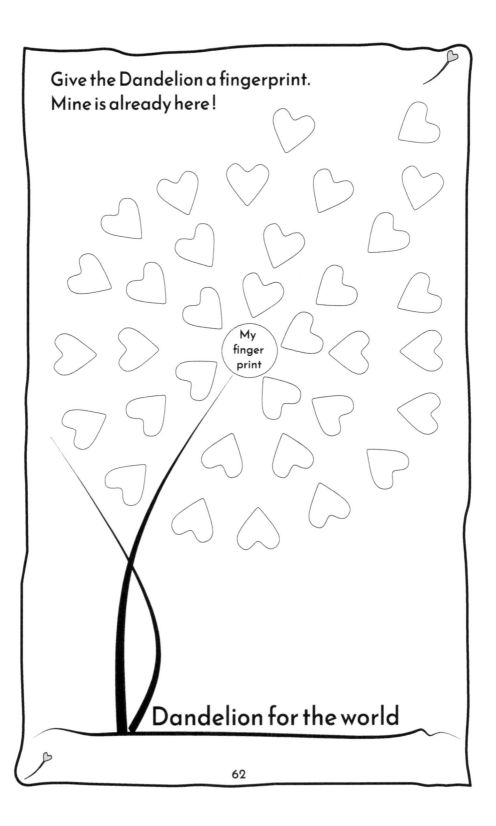

Give the Dandelion a fingerprint.
Mine is already here!

My finger print

Dandelion for the world

Lightning Source UK Ltd.
Milton Keynes UK
UKHW020728280721
387854UK00001B/21